The NEWCASTLE Cook Book

A celebration of the amazing food & drink on our doorstep.

The Newcastle Cook Book

©2016 Meze Publishing. All rights reserved.

First edition printed in 2016 in the UK.

ISBN: 978-1-910863-04-6

Compiled by: Heather Hawkins

Written by: Karen Dent

Photography by:
Marc Barker (www.marcabarker.com)
Tim Green (www.timgreenphotographer.co.uk)

Edited by: Rachel Heward, Phil Turner

Designed by: Paul Cocker

Cover art: Luke Prest, www.lukeprest.com

Contributors: Faye Bailey, Kerre Chen,
Samantha Cocker, Kelsie Marsden

Published by Meze Publishing Limited
Unit 1 Beehive Works
Milton Street
Sheffield S3 7WL
Web: www.mezepublishing.co.uk
Tel: 0114 275 7709
Email: info@mezepublishing.co.uk

FOREWORD

"People are caring more about what they buy and eat ... we now have some fantastic restaurants in Newcastle." David Coulson, Peace & Loaf.

Newcastle has improved immensely in the last five years when it comes to the quality of food, and the products people are producing are getting better all the time.

People are caring more now about what they buy and eat. I think a lot of that is probably down to travel. People go and see new things and they want it, and that has resulted in restaurants stepping up to the mark. We now have some fantastic restaurants in Newcastle.

At Peace & Loaf, we're improving all the time and we have a full restaurant every night. We add our own little twist and people enjoy what we're doing. We've been sourcing pork from Barcelona, cooking it medium-rare and people love it. It's the kind of thing that people might have had when they've been away.

Newcastle's restaurant scene is also benefiting because it's also cheaper to eat out in the city now. We have a restaurant that's for everybody, and that's something that we're seeing much more of across Newcastle. There are some great taster menus at different restaurants where it won't cost you an arm and a leg to try some truly special food. If you come for a meal at Peace & Loaf, it's cheaper than eating at a chain – and the food is so much better!

We've seen a big culture change in people's behaviour over the last few years too. Back in the 1990s, Newcastle was all about going for a drink on the Quayside. Now we're seeing the kids come out for a nice meal before they go for a drink. There's also a big trend for people to go out for a meal after work, so it's a real seven days a week industry and it's much more accessible for everyone.

Although new flavours and ingredients have added a real vibe to our eating out scene in the North East, we also have a fantastic food heritage that we shouldn't forget. There are few things better than a traditional ham and pease pudding, stottie cake sandwich or fresh fish and chips on the coast.

And there is such a wealth of great producers in the North East too, whether you're looking for vegetables, artisan bread, local meat or handmade sausages for a weekend fry-up.

There's so much in Newcastle to get your teeth into.

David Coulson

CONTENTS

WELCOME TO NEWCASTLE

Newcastle is synonymous with a great night out, and now more so than ever, that means going for a top quality meal at one of the city's fantastic restaurants.

Newcastle. A coastal city, first established on the bank of the River Tyne by the Romans and named after the castle built by William the Conqueror's son, Newcastle is bordered by Northumberland to the north and County Durham to the south. The location has played a big part in Newcastle's food heritage and today's chefs have access to fresh fish landed at North Shields as well as superb local meat from Northumberland and Durham, which are both noted livestock producing areas.

Think Newcastle food and drink, and stottie cakes and Newcastle Brown Ale spring immediately to mind. Stotties – large, round breadcakes – have been taken nationwide by Greggs, which is based in Tyneside. They're particularly good filled with ham and pease pudding, another local delicacy made from boiled and mashed yellow split peas.

Newcastle Brown Ale may no longer be made within sight of the River Tyne, but it's still one of the area's most famous brands. Today, small batch of real ale brewers and spirit distillers have picked up the baton, so quality locally-made alcoholic refreshment remains an integral part of the city's make-up.

Newcastle is also home to dishes less well-known outside of the North East. Pan Haggerty, made from sliced potatoes, cheese and onions is tasty winter warmer, and Singin' Hinnies are a sweet scone cooked on a griddle. Their name comes from the 'singing' noise they make while cooking. Craster Kippers, traditionally oak-smoked in the Northumberland fishing village of Craster, are also an important ingredient in the North East's foodie map.

Eating out in Newcastle today means a choice of cuisines from around the world. The city has a vibrant restaurant scene, including Peace & Loaf in Jesmond. The regular NE1 Restaurant Week offers the chance to try top-class venues at bargain prices.

The city's thriving tea and coffee shop culture offers some sophisticated tastes for connoisseurs and you'll find superb sweet and savoury treats on offer alongside your cuppa, from melt in the mouth cakes and brownies to belly-busting sandwiches.

In the centre of Newcastle, the Grade I listed Grainger Market is a great place to try international street food, as well as picking up the freshest ingredients for your own dishes. The Sunday Quayside market is also worth a visit for locally-sourced, artisan and homemade produce. Plus, the cosmopolitan flavour of well-stocked local delis and delicious local meats, cheeses, breads and baked goods available from North East farm shops and farmers' markets will provide the inspiration to ring the changes in some of your own meals.

The Newcastle Cook Book brings together recipes from some of the very best food and drink businesses in the city and surrounding area, offering a taste of the North East and further afield. Whether you're seeking a new twist on a traditional favourite, a cake that'll have them queuing for second helpings or want to recreate a restaurant quality dish in your own kitchen, there's a marvellous selection of recipes to tempt the tastebuds.

Dive in for inspiration and a flavour of some of the very best culinary creations the city has to offer.

Enjoy!

The authentic
TASTE OF ITALY

Two restaurants and delis bringing the sunshine flavours
of Sardinia to the North East.

With a restaurant and deli in Gosforth and a stand alone deli in Jesmond, Adriano's offers something extra to the traditional Italian restaurant.

Adriano Addis doesn't focus on the Mediterranean flavours people know so well, but puts the spotlight on Sardinian cuisine. A native of the Italian island, he's been in the UK for 40 years and comes from family that runs restaurants across the region.

He said: "This is much more regionalised food. People travel a lot more now and they are much more aware of the different regions of Italy.

"Sardinian food is known for its simplicity. The flavours aren't disguised by other things. Every dish has the taste of what it is."

Classic Sardinian recipes on the menu include suckling pig, belly pork and octopus, plus a selection of tapas, pasta and risotto dishes with a flavour of the southern Mediterranean island. The pizzas are baked in a wood-burning oven and the puddings are supplied by Gingerinos.

Adriano sources his ingredients from an Italian supplier importing Sardinian food and wines, while the meat comes from the UK. His mantra is "fresh, simple and effective" and everything is created from scratch. Diners can take home a selection of Sardinian flavours too from Adriano's delis that are packed with specialist ingredients.

The Gosforth restaurant creates a feel of rustic Sardinia inside a building that dates back to the 1700s. The semi-open kitchen means diners can enjoy the glorious scents of cooking while they wait, adding to the anticipation of their own meal. The Jesmond outlet has more of a café vibe.

Teaching people about the roots of the food and the island that inspired it is something Adriano is passionate about and his staff love answering customers' questions.

Adriano said: "We do promote the island of Sardinia. I wanted to teach people in Newcastle about this lovely island that was conquered by the Moors and has a Spanish influence.

"People don't know about it, it's a bit of a mystery – even though it's the second biggest island in the Mediterranean."

With an ambassador like Adriano, it's certain the flavours of this sunshine island will be attracting plenty of fans in Newcastle.

Adriano's
SUCKLING PIG AND PINZIMONIO

A traditional Sardinian treat to cook on the barbecue or in the oven. Serves 8-10.

Ingredients

For the sucking pig:

6kg-7kg whole pig

Lard

For the pinzimonio:

Selection of raw carrot, fennel, celery or other crunchy vegetables

Extra virgin olive oil

Balsamic vinegar

Salt

Method

For the suckling pig:

You can buy small suckling pigs online or order one through your butcher. This method is also suitable for large pieces of pork.

First, scrape the skin, scorch the bristles and wash and clean the pig.

The traditional Sardinian way to cook the pig is over a special wood fire made from holm oak and juniper, to give it a particular aroma. The meat is skewered, then placed on a rotisserie around 50cm over the fire to roast. Cook the chest first, then begin to turn the meat, dripping melted lard on to the skin to baste.

If you don't have a rotisserie, you can cook the pig outside on a tray over a barbecue or in the oven. Preheat the oven to 170°c and roast the pig for 2½-3 hours.

For the pinzimonio:

Chop the vegetables into large, chunky pieces.

Shake together the extra virgin olive oil and balsamic vinegar to make the dip and season to taste with salt.

Serve the vegetables on a large plate and the dip in a large bowl so everyone can help themselves.

Gingerino's
PROFITEROLES
WITH WARM CHOCOLATE SAUCE

A classic Italian pudding from our local pâtissier Jimmy at Gingerino's. We use Jimmy for all our desserts from Tiramisu to Chocolate Fondant - they're all amazing. Serves 8.

Ingredients

For the choux pastry:

125ml whole milk

125ml water

100g butter

10g sugar

Pinch of salt

150g strong flour

4 medium free range eggs

For the vanilla Chantilly cream:

600ml whipping cream

40g caster sugar

1 Madagascan vanilla pod

For the warm chocolate sauce:

500ml double cream

200g 54% cocoa or higher dark chocolate, chopped very small

50ml alcoholic spirit or liquor of choice (optional)

For the garnish:

25g pistachio nuts, crushed

Method

For the choux pastry:

Preheat the oven to 220°c.

Combine the milk, water, butter, sugar and salt in a pan and bring to the boil, ensuring the butter has melted. Remove from the heat and add the sifted flour slowly, combining with a wooden spoon.

Over a medium heat, continue beating with the wooden spoon until the paste comes away from the pan easily.

Remove the paste from the pan and lay flat on the work surface, breaking up with the side of the wooden spoon. Allow to cool for five minutes, then place the paste in a stand mixer with the beater attachment. Beat and add the eggs, one at a time, ensuring each egg is fully incorporated before adding the next. The paste should still be stiff enough to pipe.

Place the choux paste in a piping bag with a 7mm round nozzle. Line a flat baking sheet with parchment paper and pipe the paste into small rounds no bigger than the width of your thumb. Leave plenty of space between each to allow for the pastry to rise.

Place in the oven and bake for 20 minutes, then reduce the temperature to 170°c and bake for a further 5-10 minutes until evenly coloured and crisp.

Remove from the oven and transfer the pastry to a cooling rack.

For the Chantilly cream:

With a sharp knife, cut down the length of the vanilla pod and scrape out the seeds into a mixing bowl. Add the sugar and cream and whisk until firm, but don't over whip. Place into a piping bag with a filling nozzle.

Make a small incision in the cooled pastry balls with a knife and use the whipped cream to fill the balls. Refrigerate until needed.

For the warm chocolate sauce:

Bring the cream to the boil and if you are using alcohol, add it now.

Add the chopped chocolate and whisk until fully incorporated.

To serve:

The profiteroles can be served individually or placed on a decorative plate to share. Cover the profiteroles with sauce and a sprinkle of crushed pistachios.

The perfect
COMBINATION

Home to Newcastle's only gin still, Bealim House distils a fine atmosphere and great food – as well as the unique Newcastle Gin.

When it comes to locally-produced drinks, you simply can't get any better than Bealim House, where customers can enjoy Newcastle Gin distilled on the premises.

The gin still – an 8ft tall, 400 litre receptacle, hand-beaten in Portugal – can be seen while you sip your gin and sample some of the gastro food tapas on offer in the bar.

Newcastle Gin is a new drink, produced by Bealim House owners the Vaulkhard Group in collaboration with local artisan distiller, Durham Gin. It's a unique recipe and the spirit is only available in Bealim House, where it's going down a treat served with premium Fever-Tree tonic or mixed with Caribbean grapefruit-flavoured soft drink Ting.

Vaulkhard Group MD Oliver Vaulkhard said: "It's a very, very smooth gin that's lovely for people who are experimenting with gin. It's getting a fantastic reception from both gin newbies and gin connoisseurs."

The popularity of the new spirit means Bealim House is struggling to keep up with demand. Each batch of Newcastle Gin, which has hibiscus tones, is created over two days.

The 'hard' botanicals are added to alcohol first for 48 hours, then the 'soft' ones are mixed in before the five-hour distilling process begins.

Newcastle Gin isn't the only new thing about Bealim House. The former print works has been owned by the Vaulkhard family for 17 years and was previously a sports bar. But Bealim House, which opened at the end of August 2015, is a completely different concept. The interior was stripped back to reflect its previous industrial use, then furnished with comfortable vintage leather seating to create a very social environment and a friendly vibe.

The menu echoes the social feel and is created to share: small plates of gastro food tapas prepared using the best local ingredients. The menu changes throughout the year to reflect the seasons.

This fusion of Newcastle Gin, an eclectic choice of food and a fantastic atmosphere is set to be a real winner.

Bealim House
GLUTEN-FREE BEER BATTERED FISH AND CHIPS WITH MUSHY PEAS

A mouth-watering take on traditional fish and chips
using gluten-free flour and beer. Serves 4.

Ingredients

For the beer batter:

250g Doves Farm all purpose gluten free-flour

1 tsp sugar

1 tsp smoked paprika

1 tsp salt

1 tsp curry powder

½ tsp ground white pepper

1 bottle Estrella Daura

For the mushy peas:

250g peas

1 small onion, chopped

25g butter

100ml vegetable stock

100ml white wine

Salt and pepper to taste

10 mint leaves, roughly chopped

For the fish and chips:

4 x 200–225g codling or haddock fillets, whichever you prefer

2kg Maris Piper or Desiree potatoes

Method

For the beer batter:

Place all of the dry ingredients into a large mixing bowl and whisk together until thoroughly combined.

Add the Estrella Daura, mix to a smooth, lump-free consistency. If the mix is a little thick, either add a little more beer or a splash of soda water.

It's best to make the batter a good 3-4 hours before needed, to allow it to rest. Whisk quickly before use.

For the mushy peas:

Gently sauté the onions in the butter until tender.

Add the peas and the rest of the ingredients and bring to the boil. Reduce to a simmer for 10 minutes.

Remove from the heat and place in a food processor and blitz gently to break down (but not purée) the peas. Alternatively, use a potato masher.

For the fish and chips:

Wash and cut the potatoes into chips. Leaving the skins on adds so much flavour and they look great.

In a deep fat fryer, blanch the chips on a low heat of 135°c for 8-10 minutes or until tender, then leave to drain.

Season the fish with fresh ground pepper and sea salt. Lightly dust with gluten-free flour, then dip into the batter mix.

Increase the oil heat to 180°c, then slowly place the fish into the oil one at a time, waving them back and forth, so they don't sink to the bottom and stick.

Cook for approximately 5 minutes, then place on kitchen towel to remove excess oil. Keep warm in the oven while the chips are cooking.

Drop the chips back into the hot oil for approximately 2-3 minutes until nice and crispy. Season with sea salt.

To serve:

Share the chips onto four plates and top with the fish. Finish with a ramekin of the mushy peas, tartar sauce, a wedge of lemon and a nice cold bottle of Estrella Daura.

All ABOARD

A taste of the sea, and much more,
in this coastal café where dogs are welcome too.

For top local scran by the coast, The Boatyard is the venue of choice for Tynesiders in the know. Tucked just around the corner from Cullercoats Bay, this café-come-bistro serves fresh locally sourced dishes, created using organic and free-range ingredients.

Boasting an evolving menu it attracts an eclectic mix of foodies and locals. From early risers hankering after the alternative vegetarian breakfast to dog walkers dropping in for a coffee with their four-legged pals, all are welcome aboard.

Cullercoats-born Tom swapped cooking at high-end ski chalets in the French Alps for life in the bay when he opened in 2015. Formerly the well-loved Copper Kettle he transformed it into a smart and modern eatery that opens for breakfast and lunch. Service continues into the evening with fine wines, Cullercoats Brewery beers and bespoke cocktails.

Natural tones and rustic decor mirrors the heritage of the fishing village, with images of fishwives and beach-goers from decades past adding to its local charm.

"We work with some fantastic suppliers whose great produce lets us celebrate the best foods that the North East has to offer. We're proud of the rich culinary history of our region and reflect it in our seasonally changing menu that can include anything from home-roasted ham and pease pudding stotties to North Shields Fish Quay cod and thrice-cooked chips" says Tom.

The café is renowned for its signature Boatyard Blend of coffee, specially created by York Coffee Emporium from Malawian Pamwamba beans. Having spent a portion of his childhood in Africa, Tom donates a percentage of profits from each cup to the Friends of Malawi charity.

"We've tried to create a place where everyone in the community feels welcome. Though food is central to our ethos we want The Boatyard Kitchen to be a place where people can come together, enjoy themselves and connect. We also offer live music nights and a hub where artists and locals can mix for a bite and an evening tipple and get a real taste of the Geordie coast."

The Boatyard Kitchen

The Boatyard Kitchen
GLAMORGAN SAUSAGES

Tasty homemade vegetarian sausages that make the ideal centrepiece for a healthy but substantial breakfast. Makes 10.

Ingredients

2 medium leeks, chopped

1 red onion, diced

25g butter

200g mature cheddar, grated

200g fresh breadcrumbs

¼ tsp grated nutmeg

¼ tsp ground cumin

1 tsp wholegrain mustard

Handful fresh parsley

1 tbsp thyme

Pinch of salt and pepper

2 eggs, beaten

Flour

Vegetable oil for frying

Method

Melt the butter in a pan and sauté leeks and onion for around 5 minutes until slightly softened.

Add the herbs, spices and seasoning and cook for a further minute. Remove from the heat and leave to cool for 15 minutes.

When cooled, add the mustard, cheddar and 100g of the breadcrumbs. Mix then chill in the fridge for an hour.

Form the mixture into sausage shapes. Roll first in the flour, then egg, then the rest of the breadcrumbs until fully coated.

Cook the sausages in hot vegetable oil for 4-5 minutes, until golden brown, or shallow fry for 2 minutes each side and transfer to oven until hot throughout (around 10 minutes).

For an alternative Boatyard Breakfast, serve with grilled halloumi, roast tomato, field mushroom, wilted spinach and a poached egg.

Glamorgan sausages can be kept in fridge for up to 3 days.

ORK
OFFEE
PORIUM

e Blend

t and
s mocha
ngering
rtaste

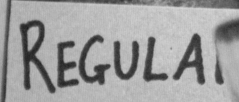
REGULA

LARGE.

Know YOUR SALT?

Traditional North Shields smoking techniques produce a range of flavours that add a new dimension to dinner.

A taste of continental cookery mixed with the traditions of the North East coast is encapsulated in the smoked taste of Boulevard Creative Cuisine's products.

Smoked salts, peppercorns, oils and dried mushrooms make up the range that was launched by Audrey Grieve, a former pharmaceuticals managing director, in 2012.

She said: "I've gone from international company director to barrow boy in three years."

The concept of Boulevard Creative Cuisine came from Audrey's extensive travels in her previous career, which took her across Europe. She was introduced to smoked salt by colleagues in Paris, and on returning to the UK to live in North Shields, she was disappointed that she couldn't buy anything of the same quality in Britain.

"I live right on the river in North Shields and I was sitting one night, thinking what is North Shields famous for?" she said.

"There were 13 smokehouses in its heyday. The oldest started in 1883. I got hold of the old boy who had the oldest smokehouse, and said why don't we make our own? He said it'll never work."

He taught Audrey traditional smoking techniques – and fortunately was proven wrong in his assessment that her smoked salt idea wouldn't work. The smoking base did, however, have to move away from its original location on the Fish Quay to stop the salt absorbing the fishy odours in the atmosphere.

Audrey sells her range of delicious condiments and smoked mushrooms at food fairs across the North and is keen to extend her customer base to delis, farm shops, Amazon and eBay. Each starter pack of smoked garlic salt, pink pepper, garlic oil, chilli oil and smoked mushrooms contains a recipe showcasing some creative ways of using the products.

Audrey said: "It's been so well received. When people use the salt, they don't want to go back to normal salt.

"I keep saying I'm going to limit supply of the smoked garlic salt as it's so addictive. I'll put up the price and this time next year, I'll be able to buy an island!"

Boulevard Creative Cuisine
PORK FILLET WITH SMOKED MUSHROOM DUST AND WILD MUSHROOM FRICASSEE

A tasty take on pork served with homemade potato gnocchi. Serves 6.

Ingredients

For the pork fillet:

2 tenderloin pork fillets, trimmed of skin and sinew

1 packet Boulevard smoked dried mushrooms

2 tbsp Boulevard black pepper oil

For the gnocchi:

250g Desiree potatoes

30g Italian 00 flour

30g cornflour

1 egg, beaten

Salt and nutmeg to taste

For the fricassee:

50g butter

3 shallots, chopped

3 cloves garlic, chopped

400g mixed wild mushrooms, cleaned and sliced

1 tbsp parsley, chopped

1 tbsp tarragon, chopped

100ml Madeira

200ml double cream

100g young spinach leaves

120g Parmesan cheese, freshly grated

1 tsp Boulevard smoked pink peppercorns, ground

Method

For the pork

Blitz the dried mushrooms in a blender until they are dust and season with a little salt but no pepper.

Roll each piece of pork in the mushroom dust and wrap in cling film until needed. This can be done beforehand; there will be more flavour the longer you leave it in the fridge.

Pan-fry the pork fillet pieces in a little smoked pepper oil until brown and sealed then pop into a hot oven for 9 minutes. When cooked, rest the meat for another 9 minutes.

During this time, warm the plates and pop the fricassee under the grill.

Slice the pork at an angle and arrange on warm plates with a sprinkle of the dust and garnish with herbs.

Serve the fricassee as a sharing dish.

For the gnocchi

Boil the potatoes in their skins for around an hour. Scoop out the flesh, then pass through a sieve or ricer. Add the flours and egg while the potato is warm.

Roll by hand into long sausage shapes and cut into cork sized pieces or marble sized balls.

Pop into a large pan of salted boiling water a few at a time. They will sink then rise to the surface once cooked. Scoop out of the pan and drain on a cloth.

For the fricassee

Fry the shallots and garlic in the butter then add the wild mushrooms. Cook gently for 10 minutes then add the herbs.

Pour in the Madeira and bring to the boil, then add the cream. Reduce the mixture by a third and add the pink pepper.

Add the spinach and half the cheese, then stir in the gnocchi and simmer for 10 minutes. Preheat the grill.

Tip the cooked fricassee into an ovenproof dish and top with the remaining cheese.

Chocolate HEAVEN

Chocolate brownies and white chocolate blondies
with a gorgeously gooey texture are The Brownie Bar's trademark.

Started by sisters Rachael and Sarah Cawkwell in 2010, The Brownie Bar is now satisfying customers' cravings for something sweet seven days a week from its base in Newcastle's Eldon Garden.

Sarah, who worked as a pastry chef, and marketer Rachael, who had worked in product development for a chocolate company, originally started selling cupcakes at markets and events. But they spotted a gap in the market for something a bit different and started to experiment with different flavoured brownies.

The idea was a hit and the sisters gave up their jobs to concentrate on brownie baking full time. They moved from making their products in their own kitchen to their own commercial kitchen in 2012, with the shop opening in 2013. Now they hand make more than 30 different varieties of brownie that are sold in Newcastle and at events nationwide.

The Brownie Bar is constantly developing new flavours and visitors to the shop can choose from mouth-watering specials every week, from triple chocolate brownies to lemon meringue blondies, which are white chocolate-based. Top sellers are the salted caramel brownies and Nutella and peanut butter blondies.

Sarah, who looks after the recipes, has also created some extra special twists on the basic brownie slice. Brownie Bombs are little balls of brownie encasing a squidgy salted caramel or peanut butter centre, all wrapped up in milk chocolate, and the Corker combines a soft chocolate chip cookie with brownie mixture at the core.

The Brownie Bar's ethos is to produce top quality, handmade brownies with that all-important gooiness.

Rachael said: "We just do brownies – but we do brownies very well."

Customers can buy take-out brownies or sit down to enjoy their sweet treat with ice cream or custard, washed down with a hot drink or an ice cream milkshake. There is also a loyalty card scheme to collect brownie points towards your next slice of chocolate heaven.

THE BROWNIE BAR

THE BROWNIE BAR

The Brownie Bar
THE CORKER

A gooey brownie baked inside a chocolate chip cookie...hard to resist straight from the oven. Makes 20.

Ingredients

For the brownie:

500g caster sugar

300g unsalted butter

5 eggs

170g plain flour

100g dark chocolate

50g cocoa powder

For the cookie:

800g plain flour

500g caster sugar

400g unsalted butter

300g milk chocolate chips

200g soft dark brown sugar

5 eggs

1 tsp vanilla essence

1 tsp bicarbonate of soda

Pinch of salt

Method

For the brownie:

Place the butter in a pan and melt over a low heat. Once melted, add the sugar and stir until dissolved, then add the chocolate and stir until melted.

In a bowl, whisk the eggs, add butter mixture and whisk, then add flour and cocoa powder and whisk again.

Place on a lined baking tray and bake at 150°c for 30 minutes or until just wobbly in the middle. Leave to cool.

For the cookie:

Cream the butter and sugars in a bowl, add the eggs and vanilla essence and whisk. Add the flour, bicarbonate of soda and salt to form a dough, then fold in the chocolate chips.

To make The Corker:

Cut the brownies into small squares (we use a quarter of a brownie). Take a golf ball-sized piece of cookie mixture, flatten it in your hands and place the brownie in the centre, then wrap the cookie mixture around the brownie until you can't see it.

Place on a baking tray and bake at 170°c for 10 minutes.

Once UPON A TIME....

Tea, coffee and the most scrumptious homemade cakes aren't just a daylight treat at Cake Stories, where late night opening brings a special twist to the coffee house experience.

Cakes infused with love and care by a mother-and-daughter baking team may be the essence of Cake Stories, but there's a bigger vision at the heart of this very special shop.

"We're more about people – cake is just the excuse!" says Hannah Evans, who runs Cake Stories with her mum Liz Ward, husband Ben and father Jon. "We want this to be a place that does people good, where our customers and our team know how valued they are. We're big on family and on people's stories, which is where our name came from. A few regulars have actually become really good friends."

Cake Stories is certainly a great place to cosy in and enjoy the full cakery experience. There's so much to delight the senses - from the mouthwatering scent of fresh bakes wafting from the kitchen to the taste of the delectable artisan cakes, quirkily displayed in vintage furniture and presented on china plates. There is a growing selection of more than 30 different loose-leaf teas to choose from and the craft coffee menu uses Cake Stories' unique house blend, roasted in Yorkshire from top quality Arabica beans.

Hannah and Liz's own cake story began a few years ago. Liz trained in and started making bespoke cakes when Hannah was very small, so cakes and cake decorating became part of both of their lives. Fast forward to 2012 when they joined forces to make wedding cakes and bake for special events, it was only a matter of time before they would open a place

together. Although Hannah is a trained musician and, until recently, Liz worked with a firm of accountants, they think they've found their true calling since opening the shop in 2015.

Alongside a tempting breakfast and lunch menu, the cakes are the real stars of the show, as you'd expect. A wide selection is served including red velvet, messy oreo, carrot and orange, zesty lemon and salted caramel, plus cupcakes, brownies, and sweet and savoury scones. But there's always something different on the menu, with special flavours of the week such as courgette and apricot or gingerbread latte, and seasonal cakes that are fruity and light in the summer and spicy and warming in winter.

Hannah said: "We're always developing new recipes and we try to source our ingredients locally. We have a local farm shop supplier and we use the freshest ingredients for our entire menu. The cakes are hand-baked and decorated every day on-site and the savoury food is always made to order. We think it adds the extra 'yum'!"

During the day, Cake Stories attracts a huge mix of customers from students and business people to parents and toddlers. At night, there is "lots of laughing. It's really chilled, and everyone seems to always enjoy themselves here" says Hannah. With its comfy chairs, exposed brickwork and beautiful lighting, it's the perfect place, really, to start your own cake story...

Lunches: 11:30am - 2:30pm

TO ALLOW THE KITCHEN TO BAKE MORE CAKES

But ask anyway as we may be able

to make an exception and, after all.

SHY BAIRNS GET NOWT!

Cake Stories
SALTED TOFFEE POPCORN CAKE

A blend of moist, silky, light sponge with rich, creamy toffee flavours and the fun of popcorn that actually pops. Serves 9-12.

Ingredients

For the sponge:

300g plain flour

1 tsp bicarbonate of soda

1 tsp baking powder

1 tsp salt

225g golden caster sugar

225g light soft brown sugar, sieved

240ml sunflower oil

2 tsp vanilla extract

2 eggs

240ml buttermilk

1 tsp white vinegar

120ml hot coffee

For the toffee buttercream:

275g salted butter

500g icing sugar

120g light brown soft sugar

120ml golden syrup

30ml double cream

2 tsp good quality vanilla extract

To decorate:

50g popping candy

200g toffee popcorn

Method

This cake is easy to make but the trick is to cook until only just baked but not raw and pasty in the middle.

Preheat the oven to 180°c or 170°c for a fan oven.

Combine and sieve the flour, bicarb, baking powder and salt. In a separate large bowl, mix together the sugars and oil.

In another bowl beat the eggs, add buttermilk and vanilla extract and mix well. Add to the sugar and oil mixture and combine. Stir in the vinegar and hot coffee.

Gradually, whisk the dry ingredients into the wet, a little at a time, just until combined. The mixture will be very runny.

Line your cake tin and pour in the mixture. This is a fragile cake so if you don't use paper you're likely to lose the edges of the cake, which will stick to the inside.

Bake for 45 minutes and then, without opening the door, shake the oven if you can, to see if the centre of the cake wobbles. If it wobbles, keep doing the same test every five minutes until the wobbling stops.

As soon as it survives the wobble test, check the centre with a skewer, which should come out greasy with a few crumbs. Take the cake out and listen to it – if you can hear a strong, constant fizz, give it another five minutes. If there are a few distant crackles and pops, it's ready.

Leave to cool, then turn out of the tin and remove the lining paper from the cake.

To decorate:

Make the buttercream by melting together 150g of the butter with the syrup and brown sugar in a pan. Simmer over a low heat until it's a deep caramel colour. Remove the pan from the heat and add the vanilla extract and cream, stirring to mix together. Remove half of the sauce (which you'll use to decorate the cake later) and set both portions aside to cool.

Beat the remaining butter with an electric mixer until it is soft and whippy. Add the icing sugar and beat, scraping the sides down intermittently. Once well combined but not too soft, add the cooled caramel and beat well for a few minutes. If it's a little dry, add a splash of milk, then stir through the popping candy.

Spread the buttercream across the top of the cake, pile popcorn on top then pour over the caramel sauce so that it oozes and dribbles down the sides.

A Beautiful LITTLE HEAVEN

A quality deli and outside catering business providing handpicked items for a real taste of something different.

For an idea born on a cruise ship, it's pretty apt that the Deli Around the Corner is just around the corner from the seafront at Tynemouth.

Based in a former traditional barbers' shop, it hadn't changed in three decades before Sue Hooper opened her foodie emporium in 2005. The deli is known for its fantastic selection of cheeses – and the spectacular, multi-tiered cheese wedding cakes it makes to order. The shop is an Aladdin's cave of delights specially chosen by Sue to bring a flavour of something different to the North East.

Sue said: "We try to supply local produce as much as possible as well as traditional deli items. The market has changed hugely over the last 10 years and it's great sourcing new products."

Sue and her husband Chad met while working on a cruise ship. They shared a love of good food, with a passion for cheese and decided to put down anchor in Tynemouth, where Chad was brought up.

A decade on, The Deli Around the Corner has developed into what Sue calls a "beautiful little heaven", where foodies can satisfy their desire for quality deli items. The shop stocks more than 50 varieties of cheese, charcuterie, superb homemade preserves and marmalade, organic fruit and vegetables, Northumberland meats and pies, and has a mouth-watering bakery and patisserie selection.

Visitors can pick up a takeaway sandwich, one of their famous homemade sausage rolls, a gourmet salad box or homemade soup, or put together a bespoke hamper to take home with them. The deli also runs an outside catering service for special events from canapés, cheese wedding cakes to a full hog roast barbecue.

This is a small independent family run business, who are passionate about what they sell. A lovely addition to the community of Tynemouth.

"A lot of our customers tell us about the products they've tried and ask us to supply them. We have lovely chats with people; we really feel we're part of the community."

The Deli Around the Corner
SPICY SWEET POTATO AND CHORIZO SOUP

An aromatic and warming soup, that's just perfect for colder days. Serves 4.

Ingredients

1kg sweet potatoes, peeled and roughly chopped

1 large onion, chopped

2 pieces (approx 2 tsp) fresh ginger, grated

½ tsp chilli powder or a dollop of chilli jam

½ tsp ground nutmeg

2 links good quality cooking chorizo sausage, diced

2 pints vegetable stock

1 can butter beans

Method

Sauté the diced chorizo sausage and the onions in a pan until softened. As long as you are using cooking chorizo, you won't need to add any additional oil as the sausages will produce a rich paprika oil on cooking. Add the chilli powder and nutmeg and cook for a further 2 minutes.

Add the chopped sweet potatoes to the pan, ensuring they are coated with the chilli powder and nutmeg. Add the stock and simmer for approximately 30 minutes or until the sweet potatoes are cooked.

Either blitz or purée the soup at this stage or gently mash depending whether you want a smooth or chunky soup. If using chilli jam, add a dollop now.

Add the drained butter beans and simmer for a further 10 minutes.

Serve with warm crusty bread and garnish with a slice of chorizo.

IPA

SWITCH 51

WORKIE TICKET

BIER

BADGIE GADGIE

IPA

20

TAWNY DEE

TAWNY DEE

RUBY DUM

RUBY DUM

DRY WHITE

JACK'S PREMIUM GIN

TONIC WATER

Lovely nibble with a glass of wine or a g... Little gift for a friend...

OLIVES ET-AL

OLIVES ET-AL

OLIVES ET-AL

nairns oatcakes

FINE ENGLISH

Stag

OLIVES ET-AL

OLIVES ET-AL

BASIL & GARLIC

Loison

Loison

I'M local

Hidden Grange

Hidden Grange

Hidden Grange

Hidden Grange

Hidden Grange

Hidden Grange

Hidden Grange

ACETO BALSAMICO

Tracklements

Tracklements

Tracklements

Tracklements

Tracklements

Tracklements

Tastes from around
THE GLOBE

Global flavours meet local ingredients in a café and patisserie
that's a sweet and savoury delight.

Known for its immense breakfast menu and huge choice of mouth-watering cakes, Dil & the Bear also has a reputation for amazing attention to detail.

Just about everything on offer in the Tynemouth café and patisserie is created on the premises, whether that's the homemade baked beans in molasses and tomato sauce, the salmon cured in citrus vodka and treacle, or the cult cake truffles dipped in chocolate.

The menu brings global flavours together with local ingredients. It offers a fresh take on the combination of regional and international flavours.

"I've travelled widely and have friends from all over the world. This, together with the input from our team of chefs creates a seasonal menu which is a little out of the ordinary." says Dil.

"We make everything from our own hummus and sauces, to breads and of course the cakes. We try and source all of our ingredients from local suppliers for freshness as well as to support our local producers."

The daughter of a Cuban mother and Byker-born father, Dil lived and worked between the North East and Dubai for more than two decades before deciding to put down roots in Tynemouth where her mother had settled. Before Dil & the Bear, she ran a catering business in Dubai and is by trade an interior designer. That creative touch and desire for comfort is apparent throughout the café, from its enticing display of cakes, to the welcoming and stylish vibe inside.

With a menu that changes three to four times a year to make the most of fresh, seasonal produce, Dil & the Bear offers a huge choice of sweet and savoury dishes. Breakfasts – including vegetarian options – and lunches each take up a page of the menu and the cake selection is incredible.

"We're known for our birthday cake truffles dipped in white chocolate and topped with multi-coloured sprinkles and sweets. We also make carrot cake truffles, red velvet cake truffles, as well as several other delicious flavours."

The business sells cakes to order from their "Cakeaway" menu to take home and is also expanding its outside catering division, spreading its taste of gorgeous global flavours further across the North East.

Dil & the Bear

MACARONI CHEESE TOPPED WITH ROAST VEGETABLES, BACON CRUMB AND PARMESAN TUILLE

Warming comfort food that's certain to bring a smile to your face. Serves 4.

Ingredients

400g macaroni pasta

180g mature cheddar cheese, grated

60g butter

60g plain flour

700ml whole milk

Salt and pepper

For the topping:

120g broccoli, diced into tiny florets

120g red peppers

120g red onion

120g aubergine

120g courgette

80g butternut squash

4 rashers smoked bacon

Virgin olive oil

For the Parmesan tuille:

20g Parmesan, finely grated

Method

Dice all the vegetables to a similar size, toss in a little virgin olive oil to coat, and season with salt and pepper. Roast in the oven at 180°c for 10-15 minutes until softened and slightly caramelised, but with a little bite.

At the same time, oven-cook the bacon until crisp and golden. Remove the bacon from the oven, let it cool slightly and dice to a fine crumb.

While the vegetables are in the oven, add a large teaspoon of salt to a large pan of water and cook the pasta until it is al dente. Drain and set aside.

For the Parmesan tuille

Line a roasting tray with baking parchment and divide the finely grated Parmesan cheese equally into four rounds. Bake at 180°c for five minutes until golden. Remove from the oven, leaving to cool and crisp for five minutes.

For the cheese sauce

Melt the butter in a pan, add the flour and stir until it comes together. Add the milk a little at a time, making sure that it is well incorporated and the sauce is smooth and creamy. Season with salt and pepper, then add the grated cheddar cheese and mix well until thoroughly combined.

To serve

Add the cheese sauce to the macaroni, mix well and divide between four bowls. Top with a mixture of roast vegetables, bacon crumb and finally top with a Parmesan tuille.

Simply SUPERB COFFEE

Follow a fairy light-strewn spiral staircase down to the coffee connoisseur's paradise that is Flat Caps Coffee.

If you're seeking the perfect cup of coffee, you can't go wrong with Flat Caps Coffee. Owner Joe Meagher is the 2013, 2014 and 2015 Northern Barista champion and serving the highest standard of coffee is the shop's raison d'etre.

Hidden away, yet very close to the city centre shops, Flat Caps offers a completely different atmosphere where you can relax and let the stress of shopping melt away while you sip a cup of top quality coffee.

Customers can choose from a minimum of three different seasonal guest coffees that change with the time of year and pick their preferred brewing method: espresso, Kalita filtered, Aeropress or Syphon. If you're a real coffee connoisseur, there is also the cold-drip method which uses cold water and takes six hours to prepare.

"We're constantly striving to improve," says Joe, who is also involved in pioneering industry research to find out the best way to brew and serve different types of coffee.

Although he's at the forefront of coffee culture, former bank worker Joe used to drink instant coffee with milk and sugar in the office before setting up his shop in 2010. He trained with Pumphreys Coffee in Newcastle and Flat Caps' focus is on serving a cup of coffee that is "the best it can possibly be". As well as Joe's best barista titles, he has also won numerous awards for the quality of the espressos and cappuccinos he creates.

People come to Flat Caps for the coffee and stay for the atmosphere. Joe has worked hard to create an ambience where customers "feel they're somewhere special and different".

Flat Caps also serves up a range of teas, hot chocolate and cold drinks to enjoy with cake, soup, sandwiches and light bites such as poached eggs on toast. A favourite on the menu is the shooter sandwich, created from salt beef, chorizo, three cheeses, mustard and pickles, which is squashed overnight, then served grilled.

3 Coffees to

1) Cult of
Work Shop
Tasting no
dark choco
candied c

2) Noel
Has Bean
Tasting

Choose From

one

ffee
es - Orange rind,
ate, macadamia,
estnut.

nquisivi - Bolivia

Coffee
notes - White wine
gentle jasmine, su

The GRAINGER MARKET

Classic and contemporary all under one roof.

Located in the heart of Newcastle, the Grainger Market has been an important part of the city's shopping experience for almost two centuries. This Grade I Listed market retains much of the stunning light and airy architecture designed by John Dobson as part of the architect, Richard Grainger's redevelopment of the city in the 1830s. Grainger was said to "have found Newcastle of bricks and timber and left it in stone, stone that still stands today".

The Grainger Market opened in 1835 and is one of the few market halls that remains in use for its original purpose.

The opening was a huge celebration with a banquet for 2,000 people. There is a picture of the banquet in the Laing Art Gallery showing the arcade set with tables, with all of the men eating and the women watching the celebrations from a specially erected balcony as they were not permitted to attend. The 19th Century Grainger Market was more than a place to shop, it was also a place that people went to see and be seen.

Originally a food market concentrating on fresh meat, fruit and vegetables, the four main alleyways were initially occupied entirely by butchers. The glazed and domed arcade, which was once home to two fountains, was filled on Saturdays by local fruit and vegetable growers selling their produce from trestle tables. Today meat, fish, fruit and vegetables remain a core part of the market's offer. In addition you can find street food and cafés, fashion retailers and cobblers, pet supplies, gifts and even a stonemason among the traders selling Monday to Saturday from the market.

Today, a number of 21st Century businesses trade from market units that are not too far removed from those the first traders of 1835 would have occupied. Julien Poulalion, owner of La Petite Creperie said "We're proud to be part of such an iconic venue, right in the heart of the city. The Grainger Market's authenticity reminds us of the atmosphere in traditional French markets. It was clear to us that this was the only place we wanted to be".

The modern Grainger Market enjoys a light, bright, vibrant and buzzing atmosphere. Achieving a balance between the market's heritage and the needs of a new generation of shoppers and traders isn't always easy, but it's fair to say the Grainger Market's getting it right. Alongside craft stalls, mini bazaars, jewellers and florists, you can find high quality butchers, artisan bakers, green grocers as well as street food traders, coffee shops and cafés; there's something for everyone to enjoy.

Cllr David Stockdale, Cabinet Member for Communities and Facilities said, "The Grainger Market is a Geordie institution that we can all be proud of. It's vibrant atmosphere and friendly traders make for a real shopping experience. Whether you're a foodie or fashion conscious there's something for everyone and it's all under one roof."

One Newcastle resident wrote a message for the Grainger Market 180th Anniversary "Thank you for feeding me for a decade, cheap when I needed it most, delicious when I can afford the finest, first and always honest trade and common decency. Long may this place have another 100 years on its score to help all those who need it".

Grainger Market
STREET FOOD

An international mix of street food at its finest.

The Grainger Market isn't just somewhere to pick up fresh and affordable ingredients, it also has street food, cafés and takeaways offering an international mix of cuisines.

The businesses range from long-established Newcastle companies such as Pumphrey's Coffee and Mark Toney, who are renowned for their homemade Italian ice-cream, to newer businesses such as Nan Bei Dumpling and Tea Bar which offers a taste of sweet and savoury dumplings and exotic teas.

The recent trend for street food takeaways is increasingly popular. You can get Turkish food from Fez Food, Italian pizza from Slice, and a Portuguese chef cooking fresh fish dishes at Lindsay's Fish to Go.

When talking about modern street food, one of the resident Frenchmen, Julien Poulalion from La Petite Creperie has a definition of a crepe from his very own dictionary: "Crêpe [krep] noun: a canny pancake made by a handsome French man". A taste of France is also supplied by the French Oven, which has a mouth-watering array of freshly baked French breads, pastries and cakes on offer.

This world of taste available under one roof doesn't ignore traditional British favourites. One 2 One serves a range of home cooked meals including favourites such as shepherd's pie, sausage rolls and yummy puddings, while Eats Café has a great menu packed with hot and cold choices. Head to Sloppy Joes Deli for a phenomenal selection of sandwiches and fillings served in wraps, flatbreads, paninis or a simple bread bun.

If cheese is your weakness you'll be spoiled for choice at Matthew's Cheese, a specialist delicatessen which brings together more than 100 different cheeses from around the world including plenty of North East varieties. The business has been running for more than 50 years and also stocks preserves, herbs and other treats to serve with your cheese board.

The Grainger Market's street food and takeaways aren't just about eating, there are also plenty of opportunities to get involved and improve your own culinary skills. Pumphrey's Coffee runs a barista course at their Brew Bar in the Arcade where you can learn the right way to brew coffee and the best equipment to use. They'll also grind your choice of coffee beans and blend your own teas. Nan Bei Dumpling and Tea Bar is getting quite a name for itself on the street food scene. They attend a lot of local food events and you can watch them prepare sweet and savoury dumplings by hand.

So whether you're just after a quick bite on the go, a sit down for a coffee and a gossip with friends, or some interesting ingredients for your own recipes, you're almost guaranteed to find what you're looking for – or discover something new.

cherry scones
85p

Grainger Market
FRUIT & VEG

A rainbow of fruit and vegetables from around the world, with traditional service and bargains every day.

Fruit and vegetable sellers have been a key part of the Grainger Market's history since it first opened its doors in 1835. Today's shoppers can enjoy picking the freshest of produce from sellers around the market including Hutchinson's and TE Liddell, which are both located in the Arcade, the original home of the fruit and vegetable sellers. In the main alleys, Bryan Muers & Son, Hutton & Oliver and Hector Hall run large stalls showcasing a rainbow of in-season fresh fruit and vegetables.

Buying fresh produce at the Grainger Market is a totally different experience to picking up pre-packed fruit and vegetables at the supermarket. The Grainger Market's fruit and vegetable stalls are a visual feast of colour and texture and there are plenty of bargains to be had every day of the week.

Barry Armstrong from Bryan Muers & Son, who has over 30 years' experience in the trade, says "Our produce is fresh, straight from the box to our customers with no-one in-between. We are a strong believer in seasonal fruit and vegetables, there's a correct season for everything and we know when it's best to be picked and best to be eaten".

Traders know their customers very well and they know their regulars by name. There's a huge camaraderie in the Grainger Market and people love the friendly customer service.

Some of the fruit and veg stalls are self-service, while at others staff will take your order just as their predecessors did nearly 200 years ago. This traditional way of serving is one of the highlights of shopping in the Grainger Market but a trip to the market is also a greener, more sustainable, and economical way to shop. In the Grainger Market you can buy the quantity you want and you won't end up with lots of unnecessary packaging either.

Buying fresh from the market means you are also supporting family businesses, many of which have traded for generations and that means shoppers can benefit from the knowledge and advice of traders who really know their onions.

LEMONS

Grainger Market
MEAT & FISH

Fresh meat from traditional butchers with years of experience, and a fabulous choice of locally caught fish.

Shoppers can come in and ask for a particular cut of meat and it is prepared there and then in front of them. Buying meat from a butcher who uses traditional skills is a far cry from buying cuts of meat that have been pre-packed at the supermarket, and you can ask advice on the best cut to use in a particular dish.

You'll also be able to pick up some more unusual ingredients to experiment with, such as in-season game birds, guinea fowl or offal. Visiting the Grainger Market's butchers is a real education that can lead to a whole new approach to meal times.

Many traditional butchers have disappeared from the high street in recent years and the Grainger Market hasn't escaped the loss of some of its older butchery stalls. Finlays Quality Butchers who have been in the market for over 100 years bring in their English and locally sourced meats which are then boned and rolled on the premises.

Northumberland Sausage Company is a relatively recent addition to the market. They can create bespoke sausages for customers and run special sausage-making workshops for people who want to create their own. The company started their days in a tiny butcher's shop in Wark, Northumberland and attended street markets before coming to the Grainger Market.

Finally, a fresh food market this close to the sea wouldn't be complete without its complement of fishmongers. Chirton Fisheries, Lindsay Brothers and Lin's Seafood all occupy neighbouring units in Alley 1. They sell the pick of the day's catch from the North Shields Fish Quay and you can always find a bargain. Paul Fletcher from Lindsay Brothers says "The Grainger Market has the best quality, freshest fish in the North of England. Our customers travel from far and wide to pick the freshest North Sea fish. From North Shields fish quay market to the Grainger Market in 20 minutes".

If you like your food on the go try Fish to Go, a new concept in quality takeaway fish and seafood. Anchovies to whitebait, salmon, monkfish and tiger prawns and everything in between. The choice is endless.

Fresh from THE FARM

Family-run farm shop and coffee shop
where only the freshest produce makes the cut.

With a family butchery business going back to 1926, it's fair to say that Haswell's Homer Hill Farm Shop knows a thing or two about quality meat.

The Haswell family moved into beef farming 30 years ago, and all beef sold at the shop in Houghton le Spring is reared on site. The lamb and pork is sourced as locally as possible and the shop has a turkey farmer rearing birds on its behalf for the Christmas dinner table.

The farm to fork ethos is central to Haswell's philosophy. There is a huge selection of cooked meats prepared on the premises overnight, plus homemade black pudding, pies and stuffing. And if it isn't homemade or produced, you can guarantee it won't have travelled far.

"Our milk comes from Acorn Dairy 15 miles away in Durham, we sell Durham Brewery beer, Durham Honey and Northumberland cheeses. We source as locally as we can," says Joanne Moran, who runs the farm shop and adjoining coffee shop.

Based in a converted cowshed that retains its rustic feel inside and out, the coffee shop has been extended twice since it opened. Everything apart from the crumpets and bread buns for the bacon and sausage sandwiches are homemade – and that's just because the kitchen has such a high demand for its hugely-popular all day breakfasts.

Joanne, whose great-grandfather started the business, said: "There are six of us in the kitchen and our four chefs are all restaurant-trained."

The eclectic menu includes treats such as triple-fried chips and is strong on delicious meat dishes, as you would expect, but there are also plenty of vegetarian options, sandwiches and sweet treats too. Homemade chutneys and jams add another delicious dimension.

The coffee shop is a real social hub locally, with some regulars calling in five or six times a week to meet up with friends. But even if you don't live locally, it's worth the trip to stock up on the freshest ingredients from the farm shop and be inspired by some of the mouth-watering dishes this local produce champion creates from them.

Homer Hill Farm Shop

BEEF SHIN PIE WITH DURHAM WHITE STOUT & BONE MARROW

Slow-cooked beef, thick gravy and suet pastry combine to create the perfect pie.
Serves 4-6.

Ingredients

For the pie crust:

600g plain flour

200g beef suet, fresh if possible

120g cold butter

120ml ice cold water

2 egg yolks

12g salt

1 tbsp thyme, finely chopped

For the pie filling:

1.5kg beef shin, bone in

500ml Durham Brewery White Stout

500ml really good beef stock

200g pancetta lardons

2 large carrots, cut into 1cm pieces

1 large onion, finely diced

2 cloves garlic, minced

2 sticks celery, finely chopped

2tbsp thyme, chopped

3tbsp red wine vinegar

1 star anise

Plain flour for dusting

8 chestnut mushrooms, sliced

Salt and pepper

7cm piece of marrow bone

Method

For the pastry: (Make the pastry the day before.)

Sieve the flour into a bowl with salt and add the thyme. Rub the shredded suet and butter into the flour until it resembles coarse breadcrumbs.

Add the yolks and half the water and bring the pastry together, but don't overwork. Add more water to form a smooth, elastic dough. Shape into a round, cover in cling film and rest in the fridge overnight.

For the filling:

Season and flour the beef shin and seal in a heavy casserole pan with a small amount of dripping. Remove from the pan when well-browned. Add the pancetta and sauté until slightly crisp and the fat has rendered down. Add the vegetables and gently sweat until softened, then remove everything from the pan.

Deglaze with red wine vinegar and white stout then bring to the boil, scraping the caramelised bits from the base of the pan. Place the beef shin, pancetta and softened vegetables back in the pan with star anise, thyme and stock. Cover and cook in the oven for 10 hours at 110˚c.

To assemble the pie:

Remove the cooked meat and vegetables from the gravy. Return the pan to the heat and reduce the liquid by half into a thick gravy.

Meanwhile, in a very hot pan, fry the chestnut mushrooms in a knob of butter and splash of olive oil until golden. Season and remove on to some kitchen roll.

Pull the bones from the beef shin and scoop any remaining marrow into the sauce. Break the meat into chunks and place into the pie dish with the mushrooms, vegetables and pancetta. Remove the star anise, check the gravy's seasoning and pour over the filling. Leave to cool.

Roll out the pastry to half a centimetre thick and slightly larger than the pie dish. Place the piece of marrow bone into the middle of the dish, seating it firmly on the bottom. Using yolk only, eggwash the edge of the pie dish and lay the pastry on top. Trim, then crimp with your fingers. Where the marrow bone is pushing the pastry up, make two cuts diagonally across the top and fold the resulting flaps back to reveal the bone. Thin the egg yolk with milk and brush the top.

Place on a baking tray and cook at 175˚c for roughly 40 minutes until the pastry is crisp and golden.

LAMB STEAK
£9.99 per kg

Top of THE CLASS

Newcastle College Chefs' Academy boasts superb views and even better food, cooked by the North East's next generation of top chefs.

Newcastle College Chefs' Academy really serves up something special, both from the modern a la carte menu on offer and in its fantastic concept of training the region's best chefs for the future.

Staffed by a professional head chef plus manager Dave Simpson, the Academy serves seasonal and local dishes, all cooked by students from Newcastle College. Diners can select from a lunch menu that changes fortnightly, specially-themed evenings, or book in for the popular supper club, featuring steak nights and fish and chip Fridays.

The training aspect of the venue means some extra special evenings once a month, when chefs from Newcastle's top restaurants come in to share their expertise. Although they cook and direct the students, customers enjoy their top quality meals at the Academy's usual competitive prices.

Dave Simpson says: "It's a fantastic experience for the students to improve their skills and repertoire and enhance experience for the diners.

"The food they produce is quite astonishing for the level they're at."

Based on the third floor of the college's Lifestyle building on Scotswood Road, the restaurant enjoys stunning views across the Tyne Valley. The local flavour of the relaxed dining experience is enhanced with seasonal North East produce and the Academy even runs its own farm-to-fork project. Students begin rearing a pig each September and diners enjoy the fruits of their labours in special pork tasting evenings in the spring.

The Academy also helps students further hone their skills with its own outside catering service for corporate and celebratory events.

Amateur chefs keen to improve their own cookery credentials can book into the Academy too, learning everything from bread baking for beginners to butchery mastery classes. A junior baking class for age 10 and above is incredibly popular and always has a waiting list.

Dave said: "We're an integrated and respected member of the local dining scene. We have a good solid customer base from the general public, who come to support us and enjoy fantastic food that is competitively priced."

chefs' academy
restaurant & bar

Newcastle College
OX CHEEK WITH WYLAM ROCKET ALE

Slow-cooked overnight, this hearty, meat and ale dish is served with melt in the mouth root vegetables, mash and smoked bacon with wild mushrooms. Serves 4.

Ingredients

For the ox cheek:

4 ox cheeks, trimmed of sinew

2 medium carrots, 1 medium onion and 2 sticks celery, cut into 1cm dice

1 clove garlic, chopped

1 bay leaf, 1 sprig thyme and 8 black peppercorns

1 tsp tomato paste

500ml each of Wylam Rocket ale and dark chicken or beef stock

1 tsp vegetable oil and 20g unsalted butter

Salt and pepper

For the mashed potato:

6 medium Maris Piper or Desiree potatoes, skin left on

250ml double cream

100g unsalted butter

For the parsnip purée:

250g parsnips and 80g peeled potatoes, cut into 1cm dice

500ml full fat milk

25g unsalted butter

For the roast carrots:

4 small carrots, scrubbed clean

1 tsp each of vegetable oil, 1 tsp unsalted butter and maple syrup

For the smoked bacon & wild mushrooms:

100g smoked bacon or pancetta, cut into fine lardons or 1cm dice

150g wild mushrooms, wiped clean, trimmed and sliced

25g unsalted butter

1tsp finely chopped chives

Method

For the ox cheeks

In a heavy pan, heat the oil over a medium-high heat. Season the cheeks with salt and pepper then brown on all sides. Add the butter and allow to foam, coating the cheeks in the browning butter. Remove the cheeks to a casserole dish.

Add onion, carrot and celery to the hot pan and brown. Add the garlic and cook for a minute, then add tomato paste and cook for another minute.

Add the Wylam Ale and bring to the boil, pour in the stock and bring back to the boil. Pour the liquid over the cheeks and seal the casserole dish with foil and a tight fitting lid. Cook in a low oven at 90°c for nine hours or overnight.

When ready, remove the cheeks and cover with two layers of cling film to keep warm.

Strain the liquid into a clean pan then bring to the boil and reduce to a sauce.

For the mashed potato

Bake the potatoes in their skins at 190°c for 45-50 minutes then set aside to cool.

Bring the cream and butter to the boil in a pan and simmer until thickened and reduced by half.

Halve the baked potatoes and squeeze out the flesh into a mouli or potato ricer. Transfer to a clean pan and add the cream and butter in stages, mixing well. Season.

For the parsnip purée

Cook the parsnip and potato in a pan with the milk and a pinch of salt.

Once tender, strain and reserve some of the liquid. Purée vegetables in a blender, thinning with the reserved liquor if necessary. Add the butter.

For the roast carrots

Heat vegetable oil in a non-stick pan and brown the carrots. Add the butter, allowing it to foam but not burn.

Place the carrots in an ovenproof dish, drizzle with maple syrup and roast at 190°c for approximately 35 minutes.

For the smoked bacon and wild mushrooms

Allow the smoked bacon or pancetta to colour in a non-stick pan over a medium heat, slowly rendering some fat. When the golden brown, add butter then the mushrooms and turn up the heat. Sauté for 2-3 minutes, season and add the chives.

To serve

Warm the ox cheeks in a low oven and gently reheat the sauce. Pipe the potatoes onto warmed plates and place ox cheeks alongside. Garnish with the side dishes and sauce.

CHARRED TENDERSTEM BROCCOLI COLSTON BASSETT STILTON, BAKED QUINCE AND HAZELNUTS

A vegetarian dish bursting with sweet and savoury flavours. Serves 4.

Ingredients

For the quince terrine:

100g sugar

50g butter

4 quinces

For the broccoli:

500g tenderstem broccoli

Sunflower oil

100g Colston Bassett Stilton or cheese of choice

1 firm pear

1 tbsp toasted hazelnuts

Salt and pepper

For the dressing:

50ml hazelnut oil

25ml white wine vinegar

1tsp Dijon mustard

100g mayonnaise

100ml buttermilk

50g blue cheese

Method

For the quince terrine

Peel and thinly slice the quince using a sharp knife or a mandoline.

Heat the butter and sugar together to make a light caramel, then pour into a terrine mould or baking dish and allow to cool.

Arrange the quince on top of the caramel in even layers, then cover with tin foil and bake at 160°c for approximately an hour until a knife can be inserted without any resistance.

Allow to cool, then press with a similar sized tray on top and leave in the fridge overnight to set.

For the broccoli

Trim the base from the broccoli and cook the bases in boiling salted water until tender. Transfer to a jug and using a hand held food blender purée the broccoli stems. Season with salt and pepper. In the same pan of boiling water, now blanch the florets for 2 minutes and then quickly plunge into iced water. Remove the remaining cooled broccoli from the water and refrigerate until needed.

Dice the cheese into half-inch pieces and set aside.

Removed the terrine from the mould, trim up and slice into strips about half an inch wide. In a non-stick pan, add the sunflower oil and heat until very hot. Add the broccoli and char on one side only, then season with salt and pepper

Place all the dressing ingredients in a blender and blitz. Season to taste.

To serve

Swipe the broccoli purée on a plate and arrange the broccoli, cheese and terrine on top. Sprinkle over the toasted hazelnuts and dress with the blue cheese and buttermilk dressing, then arrange thin slices of pear around the edges.

It's a
FAMILY AFFAIR

A little taste of Italy in the heart of Newcastle
with a feel-good continental café vibe.

When Walter Pani and his brother Roberto opened Pani's Café in 1995, it was a new concept for Newcastle – an Italian eatery that didn't sell pizza.

Originally concentrating on really great coffee, sandwiches and piadine flatbread wraps, soups, cakes and ice cream, Pani's set out to do something alternative with Italian cuisine and bring a continental buzz to the city.

Walter said: "We brought really good coffee into Newcastle; the big chains weren't there then. But we wanted to do something different so we decided on no pizza."

In the intervening years, Pani's has grown from a daytime venue to incorporate evening meals – but you still won't find any pizzas. The menu changes from café to restaurant choices at 5pm, but both offer authentic Italian food with a Sardinian flavour that reflects the family-run business' heritage.

Pani's imports its Italian ingredients from Sardinia via two companies in London and fresh, seasonal meat, seafood and vegetables are sourced locally in the North East.

The menu features Sardinian chicken, fish, shellfish vegetable dishes and pastas such as Malloreddus and Fregola, which are native to the Mediterranean island. Diners can try a taste of Sardinian wines including Vermentino and Cannonau too.

"We're very traditional and authentic," says Walter.

"We don't make up dishes that if you went to Italy no one would know what it was."

The family-feel of Pani's is absolutely genuine too. As well as Walter and Roberto, the staff also includes a number of other Pani siblings.

Walter, who initially left Sardinia to learn English at Newcastle College, says: "It's very Italian and noisy – you get the feel you are in Italy.

"Our customers are part of the family too. We have lots of loyal returning customers who come in all the time, who we call by their names and ask after their families."

Pani's Café
SARTIZZ 'E' DOMU

A simple but delicious sausage salad dish
full of the authentic flavours of Sardinia. Serves 4-5.

Ingredients

950g-1kg Sardinian pork sausage ring, available to buy at Pani's Café, or good quality Cumberland sausage

250g fresh, crisp rocket leaves

Pecorino cheese for shavings

15-20 baby new potatoes

Pitted black olives

Olive oil

Method

Place the potatoes into cold water, add a pinch of salt, bring to the boil and cook for about 20 minutes.

Preheat the oven to 180°c.

When the potatoes are ready, drain them in a sieve or colander until dry and while they are draining, place a baking tray in the oven.

Rub the sausage ring with a little olive oil. Remove the warmed baking tray from the oven, put the cooked potatoes on it and place the sausage on top of the potatoes.

Cook in the oven for 20-25 minutes depending on the thickness of the sausages.

While the sausages and potatoes are in the oven, wash the rocket and drain well, and prepare the pecorino shavings using a peeler or a grater. Place together in a bowl and add the olives.

When the sausage and potatoes are ready, remove the tray from the oven. Be careful of any juices as they'll be very hot.

Remove the sausage from the tray and place on a plate or a bowl. Drain any excess jus from the potatoes and add the potatoes to the rocket and olives, mixing to combine.

Place on a large serving plate, add the sausage to the top and sprinkle with pecorino shavings to serve.

You could also serve with toasted, crusty bread or drizzle with a balsamic reduction for extra flavour.

Fresh & Funky FINE DINING

Fresh seasonal ingredients sourced as locally as possible are turned into a quirky take on British classics at Peace & Loaf.

With a name that came to owner and chef Dave Coulson in a dream, Peace & Loaf is certainly a dream come true for serious foodies.

Dave worked with Michelin two-star winning chef Michel Roux Jr and reached the finals of the 2010 TV series of Masterchef: The Professionals, so it's fair to say he knows his onions. And like as not, those onions will have been sourced from an allotment up the road.

Using really local food is a passion of Dave's. He's evangelical about working with local businesses and the "crazy stuff" grown by his allotment supplier helps inform the exciting and innovative dishes on the daily changing menu.

"It's quite funky and cool food," says Dave. "It's fresh, local and a little bit quirky."

While the chief inspiration for the fine dining menus comes from the seasonal ingredients themselves, Dave keeps his finger on the pulse of popular culture to add fun elements to his creations. Skull motif details and Jackson Pollock splashes are among his artistic touches and he brought a taste of a night out on the town to the Boozy Sorbet of the Day with a Jagermeister and Red Bull version complete with popping candy.

Open in Jesmond since the end of 2013, Peace & Loaf stretches across three floors, each of which has a different ambience. The ground floor is quiet and perfect for watching people on the busy street outside, the middle has a lively, bustling atmosphere and the top floor enjoys views of the whole restaurant, which has a total of 55 covers.

Top quality service is just as important to Dave as the fabulous food. "We're nice people, cooking nice food, served by nice waiters," he says.

That combination of customer care, plus dishes that are beautiful to look at and even more delightful to devour, is certainly ensuring that discerning diners keep coming back for more.

Est. 1st November 2013

PEACE

black Pudding

Monkfish Ham Knuckle Minestrone, Seafood

&Loaf

Peace & Loaf
IBERICO PORK

A hearty meaty dish served with squid ink and mashed potatoes. Serves 2.

Ingredients

1 tbsp squid ink

3 pasteurised egg yolks

200ml vegetable oil, plus extra for frying

Olive oil, for frying

500g pork belly

400g Iberico pork

50g samphire

150g squid

100g chorizo, diced

200g potatoes

1 onion, chopped

1 carrot, sliced

2 sticks celery, sliced

2 bulbs garlic, chopped

1 bay leaf

Sprinkle of thyme

Method

For the pork belly

Place the pork belly, onion, carrot, celery, garlic, bay leaf and thyme in deep tray and cover with water. Cook in the oven for six hours at 120°c.

Remove the pork belly from the liquid, retaining the jus, and allow it to cool. Place the pork between two trays and press in the fridge overnight. Slice into small squares of around 1 inch.

For the squid ink

Place the egg yolks and squid ink into a thermo mix, blend for 3 minutes then slowly start adding the oil until it is all gone and the squid ink reaches a thick consistency. Leave to cool in the fridge for an hour.

To serve

Boil and mash the potatoes and keep warm.

Pan-fry the pork belly in vegetable oil until crispy, then remove from the pan and keep warm.

Pan-fry the Iberico pork in olive oil for 30 seconds on each side and remove from the pan, leaving it to rest.

Place chorizo and squid into a saucepan with 100ml jus and gently warm through.

Blanch the samphire in boiling water for 10 seconds.

Swipe the squid ink purée on base of the plate using a spoon, then add mash and the sliced Iberico pork. Place the pork belly on top of the mashed potato, add the jus and garnish with samphire.

Tea with a side order of CINEMA

Quilliam Brothers brings together top quality teas, a tasty menu and mini cinema inside a glorious Georgian building close to Newcastle University.

Inspired by the tea houses of Budapest where eldest brother Tom once ran a hostel, Quilliam Brothers brings a taste of European culture to the table, along with a choice of more than 60 different loose leaf teas and a tasty homemade menu.

As well as Tom, there are Patrick and Sam that complete the Quilliam Brothers lineup. The three brothers started out together by selling bags of tea on market stalls before opening their tea house in 2013.

The shop is based inside a Georgian building that had been empty for 50 years before Newcastle University agreed to let it to the brothers. Filled with cushioned seats to create a comfortable atmosphere, the tea house mixes the traditional with the modern: customers pay at a brass-topped counter but staff use iPad technology for the till, and the cinema seats 20 on bean bags and seats salvaged from the Theatre Royal when it was refurbished. Add a gallery, good food and proper tea served in pots to the mix and you have something rather different to the usual café.

Tea and good food are central to Quilliam Brothers. Open until midnight, but not selling alcohol, the tea house serves breakfasts including Mexican eggs, homemade granola and pastries, with specials on a Saturday; hot and cold stotties and salads at lunchtime; and baked goods all day. These are all baked in-house, with choices ranging from the mouth-watering Tunisian orange cake and chocolate banana cake to quirky twists on traditional favourites such as ginger beer scones and caramel brownies.

The tea house attracts a mixed crowd, from students and lecturers, to regulars from the nearby Civic Centre, plus shoppers and tourists.

"We wanted a venue that was welcoming, where there's no rush to finish your tea and you can chill out," says Sam Quilliam. "It's a nice environment to be in."

Quilliam Brothers

Quilliam Brothers
THE BIG Q

A big sandwich using delicious slow-cooked brisket infused with herbs and spices that's worth waiting for. Serves 6.

Ingredients

For the beef:

Glug of vegetable oil

25g beef fat (ask your butcher), finely chopped

500g good beef brisket, chopped into chunks

2 small red onions/1 large red onion, thinly sliced

2 cloves garlic, finely chopped

1 heaped tsp each of ground coriander and ground cumin

1 bay leaf

1 heaped tsp tomato paste

25ml white wine vinegar

1 tsp dark brown sugar

1 beef stock cube

½ tsp pepper and salt to taste

25ml-50ml water

For the sauce:

50g mayonnaise

25g sour cream

1 tsp English mustard

Squeeze of lemon juice

Handful dill, finely chopped

Pinch of dark brown sugar and pinch of salt/pepper to taste.

To serve:

Sour dough stottie or similar bun

Extra mature cheddar cheese and thinly sliced iceberg lettuce

Method

For the beef

Add the diced beef fat to the vegetable oil and render on high heat in an oven proof casserole pan/sauté pan.

After the fat has melted, but before it smokes, brown off the brisket. Add piece by piece, and keep turning until the meat has coloured all over. Remove the meat, leaving the fat in pan.

Reduce heat to medium. Add the onions and garlic and fry for a few minutes until slightly softened and coloured. Add the spices and bay leaves and fry for 2-3 minutes more.

Add the tomato paste, vinegar, sugar, salt, pepper and stock cube. Ensure the stock cube dissolves.

Add 25ml of water, stir, bring to boil, then add the meat cubes and any juices. Cover with foil or lid and pop in the oven at 170°c for 5 hours. Check on the meat every 1-2 hours, stirring, and adding a splash more water if getting too dry. Uncover and roast for 30 more minutes.

For the sauce

Mix all of the ingredients together, ensuring the sugar has dissolved.

To serve

Slice the bun, top with meat and grated extra mature cheese, then pop under the grill until the cheese has melted. Spread with 1tsp of sauce and add thinly sliced iceberg lettuce.

BLACK PEPPER

CINNAMON

GINGER

CLOVES

MASALA
KLASAN

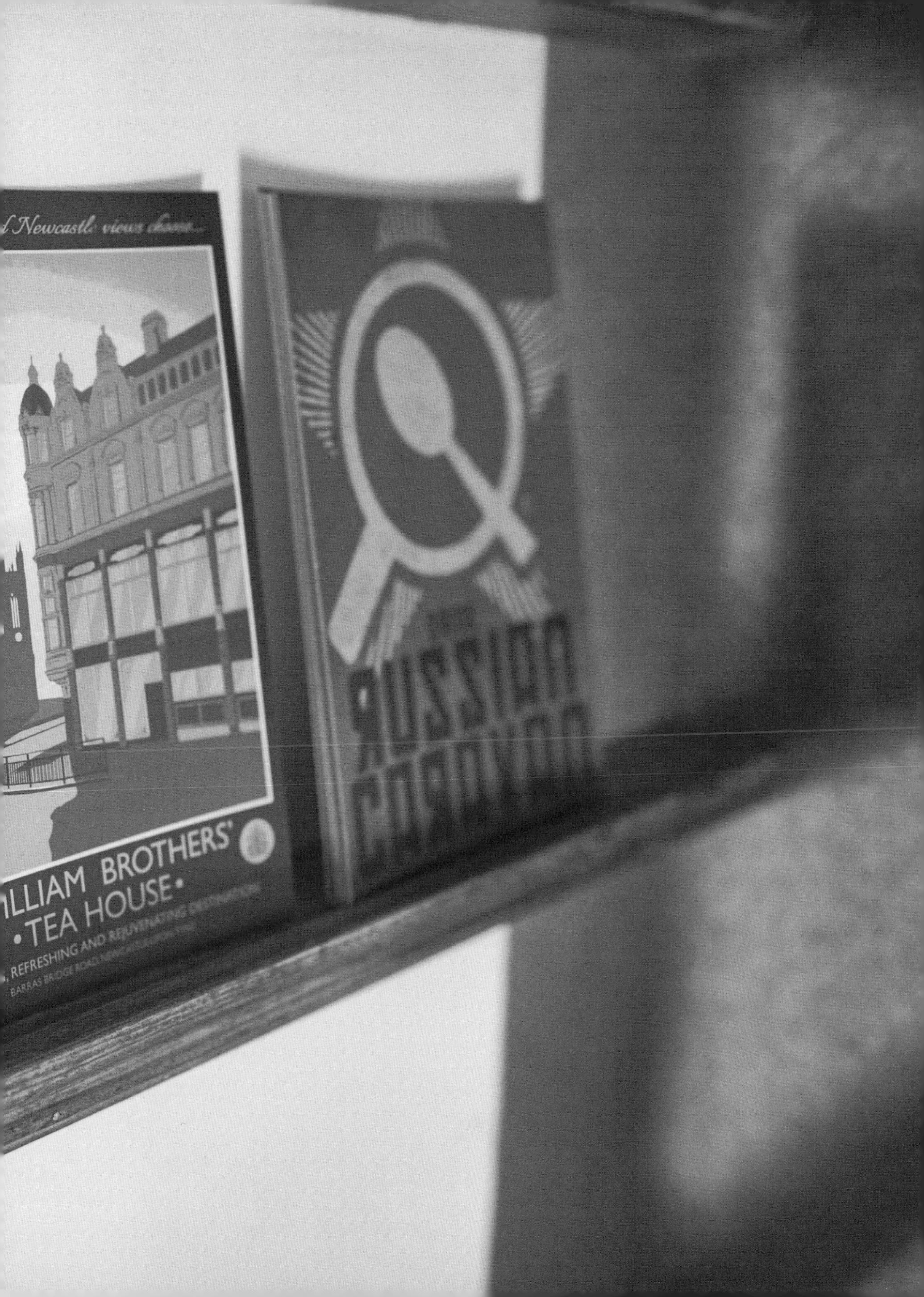
BROTHERS'
• TEA HOUSE •

Grub on THE TYNE

Sharing super-fresh tapas that's a visual as well as a taste sensation is the law of the land in this former river police station.

River Beat is overhauling diners' preconceptions of tapas with a menu infused with Asian and European delights, all freshly-prepared in the unique surroundings of a former river police station overlooking the Tyne.

Based on the Gateshead side of the river, River Beat's motto is 'obey the laws of good food and drink', and the legal connection is apparent throughout the two-storey restaurant with Banksy and American artwork on the walls to reflect the police theme. Located close to the Swing Bridge, the building includes a top-floor function room, a ground-floor restaurant and meeting room, and a relaxing outdoor eating space overlooking the river.

"The venue has an amazing ambience," says Andy Drape, a former head chef at Blackfriars Café Bar and Barn Asia, who opened River Beat in late 2015.

"Some of the views are the best in town, looking over to the Newcastle side of the river."

Andy's philosophy is to serve great food for sharing, drawing inspiration from the tapas served in Thailand, China, Japan, Korea and Vietnam, as well as the Spanish varieties people may be more familiar with.

He said: "It's fresh and vibrant and very visual on the plate. We make everything fresh, including the sauces.

"The menu's a little bit unusual with things you can't buy anywhere else. The whole idea is to serve really good, honest food that's not expensive, so people go away happy."

The tapas concept is about sharing and River Beat offers a diverse choice of large and small portions to enjoy with friends. But the restaurant also provides a range of more traditional starters and main courses for people who don't want to immerse themselves in the tapas experience, plus a kids' menu and a mouth-watering selection of desserts.

"We've got the views, the good food and the ambience," says Andy.

You can guarantee that crossing the Tyne to River Beat will certainly be an arresting experience for your senses.

River Beat

CAULIFLOWER AND HAKE FRITTERS WITH CAMBODIAN CURRY SAUCE

Tasty tapas with an Eastern flavour. Serves 6-8.

Ingredients

For the fritters:

½ a cauliflower, sliced as thinly as possible

200g hake fillets, finely chopped

2 green chillies, finely chopped

½ tsp each of chilli powder, ajwain (carom seeds), crushed, and lemon juice

2 tbsp fresh coriander, chopped

1 tsp cumin seeds, crushed

6-7 tbsp besan (chick pea flour)

2 tbsp water

Salt to taste

For the curry sauce paste:

1 lime leaf

2 lemongrass stalks, ground

1 tbsp sliced galangal, ground

2 banana shallots

4 cloves garlic, finely chopped

100g peanuts, dry roasted until toasted

1 tsp ground turmeric

1 washed red chilli, de-seeded

½ white onion

For the curry sauce gravy:

400ml coconut milk

200ml water

40ml dark soy sauce

2 tbsp honey

Salt to taste

Method

For the fritters

Put the cauliflower and the hake in a large bowl and add the green chillies, chilli powder, fresh coriander, lemon juice, cumin and ajwain. Sift the chick pea flour with the salt.

Heat plenty of oil in a deep pan to around 120°c, but don't let it get too hot. If the oil is too hot the fritters will be raw and gooey inside.

Gradually add the sifted flour to the cauliflower mixture, rubbing it in with your fingers until firm and sticky. Add the water and mix well.

Put small dollops of the mixture into the oil to fry – just a few at a time or they will be soggy. The fritters should be no bigger than 2.5cm. Fry them slowly until crisp and golden on the outside and cooked through the centre – about 3-4 minutes.

Drain in a sieve placed over a bowl and serve immediately.

For the curry sauce paste

Blend all the paste ingredients in a food processor until smooth. Heat the oil in a pan, then add the curry paste. Cook, stirring constantly for 3 minutes.

For the curry sauce gravy

To the cooked out paste, add the coconut milk, water, soy sauce and honey and bring to the boil, then reduce the heat and simmer for 10 minutes. Keep stirring every few minutes.

Serve garnished with fresh diced pineapple, red sliced chillies, crisp onion shallots and deep-fried basil.

Pop Round for SUPPER

Fresh local, seasonal food translated into menus with an international flavour at different venues around the region.

Seasonal food with a global menu and a signature starter board bringing strangers together to tuck in around a communal table are the hallmarks of the Wandering Fork Supper Club.

This moveable feast takes place three or four times a month at different venues across the North East and is a real social occasion that aims to unite diners in their love of good food. But mainly supper clubs are held in the home.

The concept came from Regional Manager Michele Deans and Jo Otter, a College Lecturer, who have channelled their foodie talents into creating an ever-changing menu, based on their own travels and the freshest ingredients available each month.

Jo said: "We have different themes, bringing together recipes from different places we've been, but they all reflect the seasons and we source the ingredients as locally as possible.

"We work with Northumbrian Heritage Meats, Alan, the owner, advises what is good and in season, and we celebrate the fruit that's in season in our puddings. Recently we put out a call on Facebook for people with plum trees to bring them round to our house and we made three different plum deserts.

"It gets people chatting about where food comes from and gets them connecting more."

The menu changes each month, and so can the venue. Sometimes the supper club is held in a diner's kitchen, on other occasions it moves to a foodie business' premises to make room for more people. The club uses its Facebook page www.facebook.com/thewanderingforkfoodcompany to keep members up to date with what's on the menu and where. Michele and Jo are also active at food festivals around the region, recruiting members to come and join in the feasts they produce.

Michele, who is a fully-trained chef, said: "We're now looking to collaborate more with local food businesses and start a cooking school.

"Jo and I love our food. We wanted to do something in our own style, with great food and a great atmosphere."

Wandering Fork Supper Club

MACADAMIA NUT CRUSTED COD
COCONUT CURRY BROTH AND SWEETCORN CROQUETTES

Served with seasonal vegetables, this seafood dish combines colour and texture
with fantastic flavour. Serves 4.

Ingredients

For the macadamia nut crusted cod:

4 x 175g cod fillets

200g salted macadamia nuts

1 tbsp butter, melted

For the coconut curry broth:

¼ tsp salt

1 onion, sliced thinly

2 cloves garlic, minced

1 tsp ginger root, grated

1 tbsp brown sugar

2 tbsp Thai red or green curry paste

1 tsp ground cumin

1 tin coconut milk

1 tbsp fish sauce

1 small bunch coriander

For the sweetcorn croquettes:

200g sweetcorn, tinned

Vegetable oil for deep frying

2 tbsp unsalted butter

2 tbsp plain flour

240ml whole milk

1 egg, slightly beaten

60g panko breadcrumbs

Salt and freshly-ground black pepper

Method

For the sweetcorn croquettes

Melt the butter in a frying pan over a medium-low heat then add flour and cook, stirring constantly, for about one minute.

Still stirring constantly, slowly add the milk. Continue to stir until no lumps remain. Raise heat to medium and cook for three or four minutes until the mixture thickens and easily coats the back of a spoon.

Remove from the heat, stir in corn and the slightly beaten egg. The residual heat will gently cook the egg. Season with salt and pepper.

Let the mixture cool completely, then place in the fridge for at least an hour or overnight.

When you're ready to cook, pour the panko into a small bowl and season with salt and pepper. Shape the corn mixture into heaped tablespoon-sized balls and coat completely in the panko breadcrumbs. Place on a lined baking tray.

Freeze the croquettes for about an hour to solidify before frying.

Heat enough vegetable oil in a pan over a medium heat (or use a deep fryer) to completely cover the croquettes. Once hot, gently lower the croquettes, a couple at a time, into the oil and fry until golden brown and crispy on all sides for 1-2 minutes.

Carefully remove with a slotted spoon on to a paper towel-lined plate to drain and cool, then sprinkle with salt.

For the coconut curry broth

Sauté the onion, garlic and ginger in a tablespoon of oil over a low heat until fragrant and the onions are soft.

Stir in the sugar, curry paste and cumin, and cook for one minute stirring constantly. Add the coconut milk and fish sauce and bring to the boil. Reduce the heat and simmer for three minutes.

For the cod

Crush the macadamia nuts and combine with melted butter. Put onto greaseproof paper to about the depth of a £1 coin and refrigerate immediately.

Steam the cod and put aside to cool.

Cut out the cold nut mixture and lay carefully on top of the cod. Preheat the grill to hot, then grill the cod until the nut mixture is browned.

Leave the cod under the lowest heat until ready to serve.

To serve

Put the coconut broth into a deep bowl, place the cod in the middle, then arrange three sweetcorn croquettes per person around the fish.

Sprinkle with fresh coriander and serve with seasonal vegetables.

The DIRECTORY

These great businesses have supported the making of this book; please support and enjoy them.

Adriano's Restaurant & Deli
90 High Street
Gosforth
Newcastle upon Tyne, NE3 1HB
Telephone 0191 284 6464
Website: www.adrianos.co.uk
32 Acorn Road
Jesmond
Newcastle upon Tyne, NE2 2DJ
Telephone: 0191 281 8188
Website: www.adrianosjesmond.co.uk
Restaurants and delis concentrating on the simple sunshine flavours of the Italian island of Sardinia.

Bealim House
17-25 Gallowgate
Newcastle upon Tyne, NE1 4SG
Telephone: 0191 221 2266
Website: www.bealimhouse.co.uk
Bar distilling Newcastle Gin on site and serving eclectic choice of gastro food tapas to share with friends.

The Boatyard Kitchen
1 John St,
Cullercoats,
Tyne & Wear, NE30 4PL
Telephone: 0191 280 1077
Website: www.facebook.com/boatyardkitchen
Seaside café with an ever-evolving menu, serving breakfasts, lunches and sweet treats.

Boulevard Creative Cuisine
22C Oak Rd.,
West Chirton Industrial Estate,
North Shields, NE29 8SF,
*NB Not open to the public.
Telephone: 0191 259 2791
Website: www.boulevardcuisine.co.uk
Innovative and flavourful range of smoked salts, peppercorns, oil and mushrooms.

The Brownie Bar
Eldon Garden Shopping Centre
Newcastle upon Tyne NE1 7RA
Telephone: 07875441274
Website: www.browniebar.co.uk
Huge variety of handmade brownies and blondies, plus brownies with a twist.

Cake Stories Coffee House & Cakery
12 Brentwood Avenue,
Jesmond,
Newcastle upon Tyne, NE2 3DH
Telephone: 07860 379249
Website: www.cakestoriesjesmond.com
Late opening cosy-rustic coffee, tea and cake shop, serving handmade artisan cakes, scones, savouries and treats with craft coffee and a large selection of loose leaf teas.

The Deli Around the Corner
61 Hotspur Street,
Tynemouth, NE30 4EE
Telephone: 0191 259 0086
Website: www.thedeliaroundthecorner.co.uk
Quality deli items from the North East and further afield, specialising in a huge cheese selection, with an outside catering service and bespoke cheese wedding cakes to order.

Dil & The Bear
18 Front Street,
Tynemouth, NE30 4DX
Telephone: 07709 178 721
Website: www.instagram.com/
dilandthebear

Café and patisserie offering a fusion of global flavours in sweet and savoury dishes made with fresh, seasonal ingredients.

Flat Caps Coffee
13 Ridley Place
Newcastle upon Tyne, NE1 8JQ
Telephone: 0191 232 7836
Website: www.flatcapscoffee.com

Award-winning coffee shop serving a choice of seasonal and guest coffees, tea, hot chocolate, cakes and snacks.

Gingerino's Patisserie
The Tower,
Uptin House, Ouseburn, Newcastle
NE2 1TZ
Telephone: 0191 265 8595
Website: www.gingerinos.co.uk

Classic patisserie selling a range of delcious sweet treats.

The Grainger Market
Grainger Street
Newcastle upon Tyne, NE1 5QQ
Telephone: 0191 211 5542
Website: www.graingermarket.org.uk

Covered market selling fresh fruit, vegetables, meat, fish, delicatessen products and a huge choice of street food, cafes and shops.

Haswell's Homer Hill Farm Shop
Pittington Road Rainton Gate,
Houghton le Spring, DH5 9RG
Telephone: 0191 584 1941
Website: www.homerhillfarmshop.com

Farm shop selling home-reared beef and locally-sourced ingredients, with adjoining coffee shop offering homemade meals, all-day breakfasts and sweet treats.

Newcastle College Chefs' Academy
Newcastle College Rye Hill Campus
Scotswood Road
Newcastle upon Tyne, NE4 7SA
Telephone: 0191 200 4602
Website: www.ncl-coll.ac.uk/lifestyle/
chefs-academy

Top quality seasonal and local meals, with special tasting evenings and super clubs, cooked by students from Newcastle College.

Pani's Café
61-65 High Bridge
Newcastle upon Tyne, NE1 6BX
Telephone: 0191 232 4366
Website: www.paniscafe.co.uk

Authentic Italian café serving lunches and evening meals, specialising in Sardinian cuisine.

Peace & Loaf
217 Jesmond Road
Newcastle upon Tyne NE2 1LA
Telephone: 0191 281 5222
Website: www.peaceandloaf.co.uk

Restaurant offering fine dining with a twist and a frequently changing menu based on local, seasonal ingredients.

Quilliam Brothers' Teahouse
1 Eldon Place,
Claremont Buildings,
Newcastle Upon Tyne NE1 7RD
Telephone: 0191 2614861
Website: www.quilliambrothers.com

Teashop serving a wide range of loose leaf tea, breakfasts, lunches and homemade baked goods, with a mini cinema and art gallery on the premises.

River Beat
Pipewellgate House
Pipewellgate
Gateshead, NE8 2BJ
Telephone: 0191 477 0553
Website: www.riverbeat.co.uk

Restaurant serving a vibrant range of fresh Asian and European tapas to share with options for starters, mains and desserts, plus kids' menu.

The Wandering Fork Supper Club
117 Kells Lane,
Low Fell,
Gateshead, NE9 5XY
Telephone: 07854 862291
Website: www.facebook.com/
thewanderingforkfoodcompany/

A moveable feast around a communal dinner table, reflecting seasonal recipes at different venues.

me:ze
PUBLISHING

Other titles in this series

The Sheffield Cook Book features
Baldwin's Omega, Nonna's, Ashoka,
Cubana, Peppercorn.
978-0-9928981-0-6

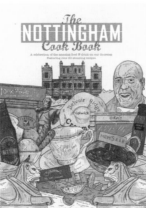

The Nottingham Cook Book features
Sat Bains with Rooms, World Service,
Harts, Escabeche
978-0-9928981-5-1

The Derbyshire Cook Book features
Chatsworth Estate, Fischers of
Baslow, Thornbridge Brewery
978-0-9928981-7-5

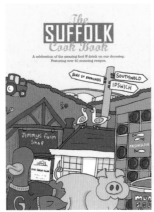

The Suffolk Cook Book features
Jimmy's Farm, Gressingham Duck,
Munchy Seeds and much more.
978-1-910863-02-2

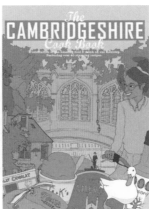

The Cambridgeshire Cook Book
features Midsummer House, The Pint
Shop, Gog Magog Hills, Clare College
978-0-9928981-9-9

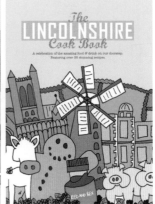

The Lincolnshire Cook Book features
Colin McGurran, TV Chef Rachel
Green, San Pietro and much more.
978-1-910863-05-3

All available from Waterstones, Amazon, independent bookshops
and all establishments featured in the book.

FIND OUT MORE ABOUT MEZE PUBLISHING AT WWW.MEZEPUBLISHING.CO.UK